LIVING WITH THE DINOSAURS

CROCODILES
LIVED WITH THE DINOSAURS!

BY MELISSA RAÉ SHOFNER

Gareth Stevens
PUBLISHING

Please visit our website, www.garethstevens.com. For a free color catalog of all our high-quality books, call toll free 1-800-542-2595 or fax 1-877-542-2596.

Cataloging-in-Publication Data

Names: Shofner, Melissa Raé.
Title: Crocodiles lived with the dinosaurs! / Melissa Raé Shofner.
Description: New York : Gareth Stevens Publishing, 2017. | Series: Living with the dinosaurs | Includes index.
Identifiers: ISBN 9781482456455 (pbk.) | ISBN 9781482456479 (library bound) | ISBN 9781482456462 (6 pack)
Subjects: LCSH: Crocodiles–Juvenile literature.
Classification: LCC QL666.C925 S56 2017 | DDC 597.98'2–dc23

First Edition

Published in 2017 by
Gareth Stevens Publishing
111 East 14th Street, Suite 349
New York, NY 10003

Copyright © 2017 Gareth Stevens Publishing

Designer: Laura Bowen
Editor: Therese Shea

Photo credits: Cover, p. 1 (crocodile) Bill Birtwhistle/Moment/Getty Images; cover, p. 1 (footprints) nemlaza/Shutterstock.com; cover, pp. 1–24 (background) Natalia Davidovich/Shutterstock.com; cover, pp. 1–24 (stone boxes) Daria Yakovleva/Shutterstock.com; p. 5 (main) Prinn Chansingthong/Shutterstock.com; p. 5 (inset) Herschel Hoffmeyer/Shutterstock.com; p. 7 (crocodile) John Kasawa/Shutterstock.com; p. 7 (velociraptor) BestGreenScreen/Shutterstock.com; p. 7 (archaeopteryx) Catmando/Shutterstock.com; p. 7 (hen) AS Food studio/Shutterstock.com; p. 9 Jason Edwards/National Geographic/Shutterstock.com; p. 11 (crocodile) Oleksandr Lysenko/Shutterstock.com; p. 13 (main) GUDKOV ANDREY/Shutterstock.com; p. 13 (spinosaurus) Valentyna Chukhlyebova/Shutterstock.com; p. 14 FunkMonk/Wikimedia Commons; p. 15 Catchlight lens/Shutterstock.com; p. 16 wildestanimal/Moment/Getty Images; p. 17 (top) underworld/Shutterstock.com; p. 17 (bottom) olena2552/Shutterstock.com; p. 19 (main) Ery Azmeer/Shutterstock.com; p. 19 (inset) De Agostini Picture Library/Getty Images; p. 20 ChameleonsEye/Shutterstock.com; p. 21 defpicture/Shutterstock.com.

All rights reserved. No part of this book may be reproduced in any form without permission in writing from the publisher, except by a reviewer.

Printed in the United States of America

CPSIA compliance information: Batch #CW17GS: For further information contact Gareth Stevens, New York, New York at 1-800-542-2595.

CONTENTS

Living with Dinosaurs 4

Ancient Relatives 6

Really Big Reptiles 8

Close to Home 10

Who's Hungry? 12

Long Lives 14

Built to Survive 16

Food for Life 18

What's Next? 20

Glossary 22

For More Information 23

Index 24

Words in the glossary appear in **bold** type the first time they are used in the text.

LIVING WITH DINOSAURS

Crocodiles have been around for a very long time. They first appeared on Earth about 200 million years ago. This means they lived with the dinosaurs! Around 65 million years ago, however, dinosaurs became extinct, or died out. Crocodiles somehow survived and are still around today.

Why didn't crocodiles go extinct? How closely **related** are crocodiles and dinosaurs? Answers can be found by studying how crocodiles have **evolved** over millions of years. We can guess what **prehistoric** crocodiles were like by learning about modern crocodiles.

THE PREHISTORIC WORLD

The prehistoric crocodile *Deinosuchus* (dy-noh-SOO-kuhs) lived between 83 million and 72 million years ago. It had sharp teeth that could smash bone.

CROCODILES AND DINOSAURS LIVED TOGETHER MILLIONS OF YEARS AGO. THE NAME *DEINOSUCHUS* COMES FROM GREEK WORDS MEANING "TERRIBLE CROCODILE."

Deinosuchus

ANCIENT RELATIVES

Crocodiles are reptiles. Reptiles are **cold-blooded** animals that have hard parts or scales on their bodies. Most lay eggs. Snakes, turtles, and lizards are also reptiles. However, crocodiles and other **crocodilians** are more closely related to birds than they are to other reptiles!

Crocodiles and dinosaurs may look alike, but they aren't directly related. Crocodiles came from animals that lived before dinosaurs. Many scientists believe that modern-day birds are directly related to dinosaurs, though. So, dinosaurs and crocodiles are like cousins!

ARCHOSAURS (AHR-KUH-SAWRZ) WERE A GROUP OF ANIMALS THAT APPEARED AROUND 250 MILLION YEARS AGO. THE GROUP BRANCHED OUT OVER TIME TO INCLUDE DINOSAURS, BIRDS, AND CROCODILES.

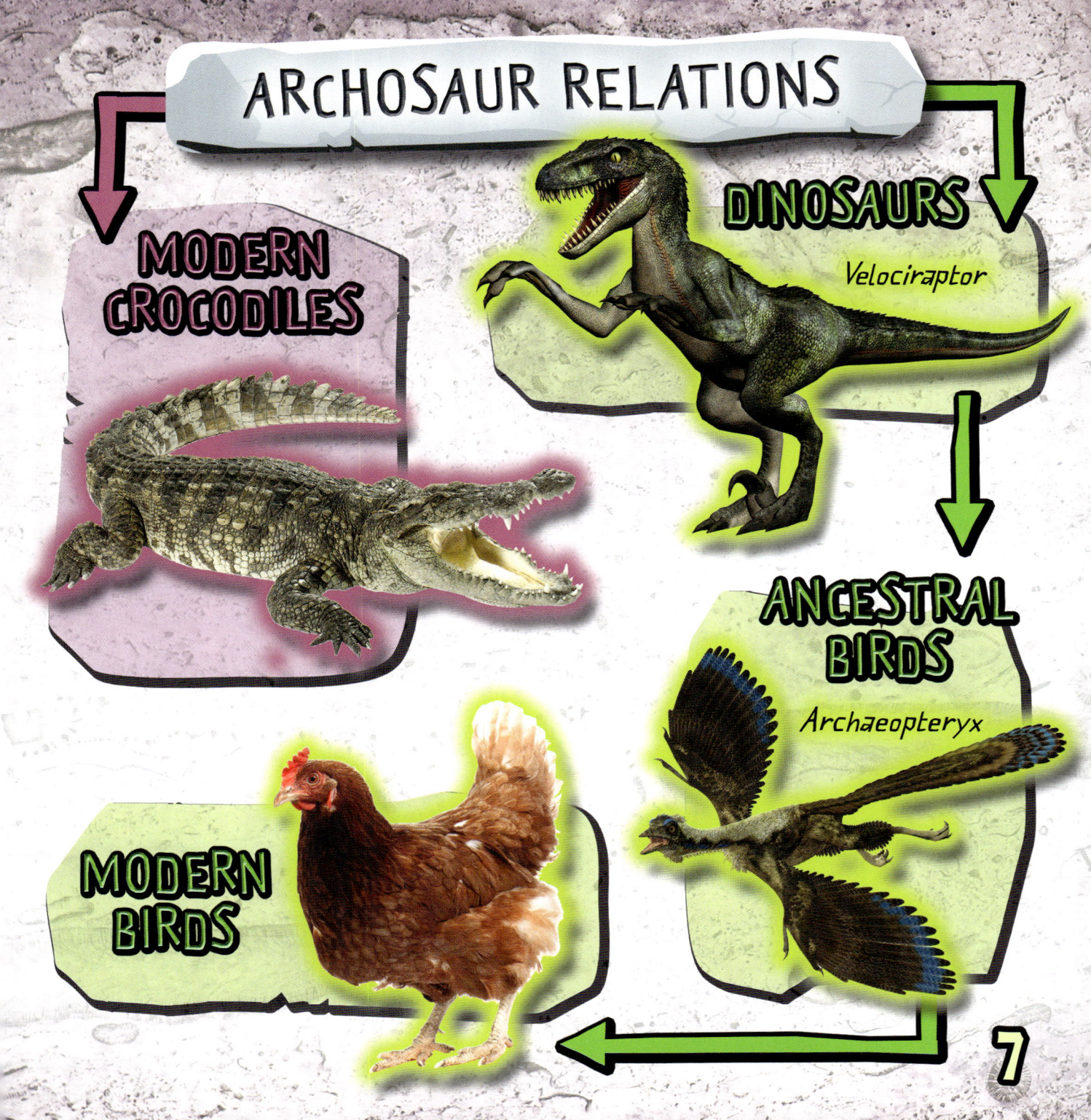

REALLY BIG REPTILES

Crocodiles have a long tail, sharp teeth, and short legs. Their snout, or nose, is long, and their **jaws** are very powerful. **Fossils** show that prehistoric crocodiles shared many of these features. Their size was hugely different than modern crocs, though!

Some species, or kinds, of modern crocodiles can grow to be 20 feet (6.1 m) long and weigh up to 2,200 pounds (998 kg). These are very large animals, but prehistoric crocodiles were even bigger. Scientists think that some were 40 feet (12.2 m) long!

THE PREHISTORIC WORLD

Sarcosuchus (sahr-koh-SOO-kuhs) was one of the largest prehistoric crocodiles. Based on fossils, scientists think that *Sarcosuchus* could have been 39 feet (12 m) long and weighed more than 8 tons (7.3 mt).

A YOUNG BOY STANDS INSIDE THE MOUTH OF THIS LIFE-SIZE MODEL OF *SARCOSUCHUS*.

CLOSE TO HOME

Crocodiles live near lakes, rivers, and **swamps**. Some, such as the American crocodile, are able to live in both freshwater and salt water. They can swim several miles out to sea and have special tongue **glands** to get rid of extra salt in their body.

Since crocodiles are cold-blooded, they live in warmer parts of North America, South America, Australia, and Asia. They're also found in Africa. Fossils of prehistoric crocodiles have been uncovered in many of the places where crocodiles live today.

THE PREHISTORIC WORLD

Rhamphosuchus (ram-foh-SOO-kuhs) was a prehistoric crocodile that lived during the Miocene period (about 23 million to 5 million years ago). It had a long, powerful tail so it could swim quickly and a narrow snout to catch fish easily.

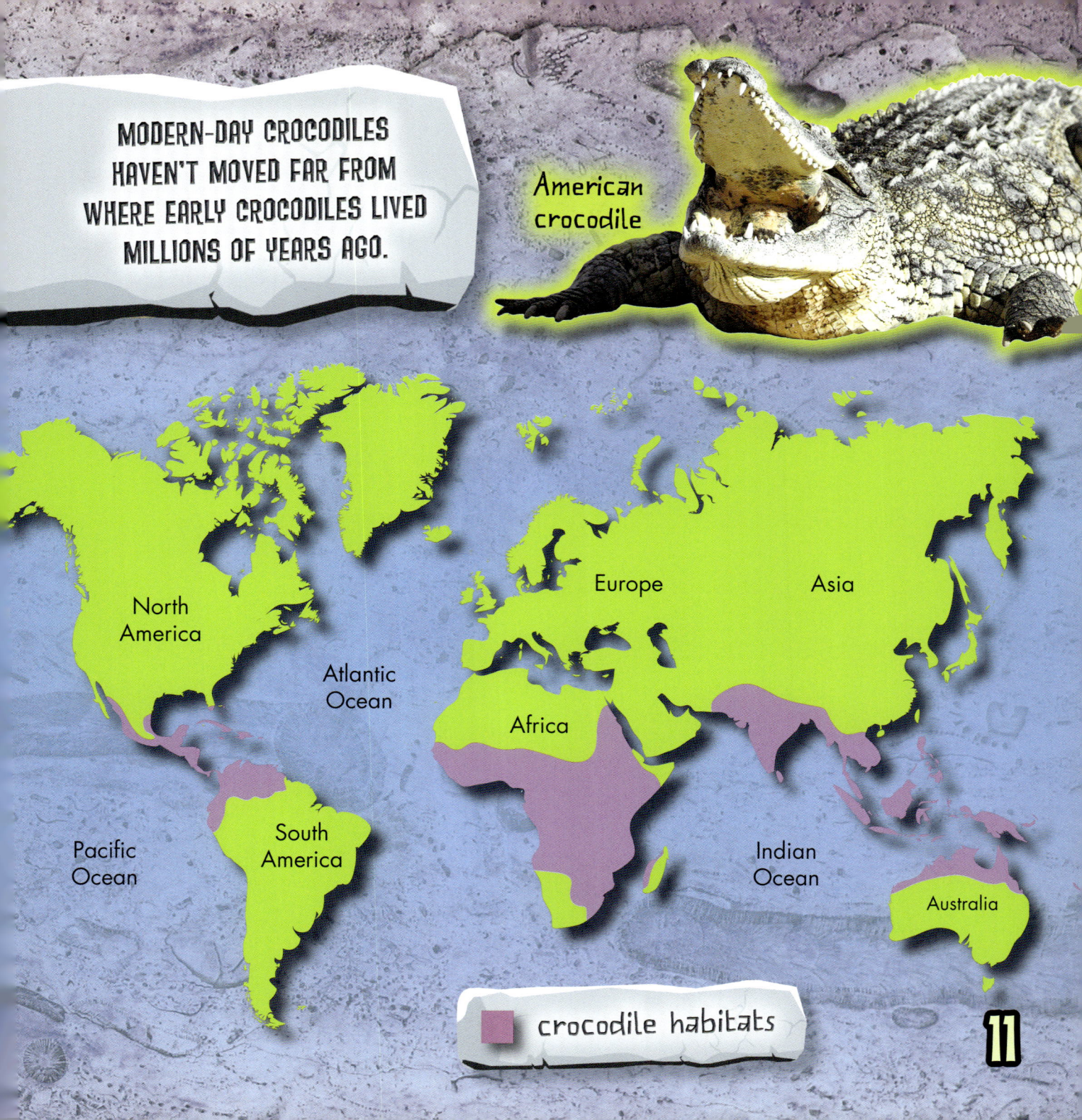

WHO'S HUNGRY?

Crocodiles are carnivores, or animals that eat only meat. Adult crocodiles eat mostly fish, but they sometimes eat birds and larger animals. Crocodiles often surprise land animals drinking at the water's edge. They drag the animals into the water and drown them. Young crocodiles eat smaller prey, such as frogs, snails, and bugs.

Crocodiles can't chew, but their jaws can easily crush prey. They eat small animals whole. They tear apart larger animals. Crocodiles swallow stones to help break down large pieces of food in their stomach!

THE PREHISTORIC WORLD

Scientists think most prehistoric crocodiles ate fish. *Mourasuchus* (moh-rah-SOO-kuhs) had a weak jaw and probably ate tiny prey. However, *Sarcosuchus* may have attacked bigger animals such as the dinosaur *Spinosaurus*.

A HUNGRY CROCODILE MAY ATTACK A LARGE LAND ANIMAL, SUCH AS A WILDEBEEST, WHILE IT'S DRINKING AT OR WALKING IN A BODY OF WATER.

Spinosaurus

LONG LIVES

Baby crocodiles are about 8 to 12 inches (20 to 30 cm) long when they first break out of their egg. They grow about 1 foot (30 cm) a year for the first 3 or 4 years. Their growth then slows, but they continue to grow for their entire life. Scientists believe that *Sarcosuchus* kept growing for its entire life, too.

In zoos, crocodiles have lived for more than 70 years. Scientists think wild crocodiles probably live just as long.

Hypsilophodon

THE PREHISTORIC WORLD

Scientists found the tooth of a small prehistoric crocodile in a fossil of a baby plant-eating dinosaur called a *Hypsilophodon* (hihp-suh-LAHF-uh-dahn). They think some prehistoric baby crocodiles may have eaten baby dinosaurs!

A MOTHER CROCODILE BUILDS A NEST TO LAY HER EGGS IN. THE TEMPERATURE OF THE NEST DECIDES IF THE BABY CROCODILES WILL BE MALE OR FEMALE.

BUILT TO SURVIVE

Scientists think early crocodiles did such a good job **adapting** to their **environment** that not much has needed to change over time. This might be why crocodiles survived when the dinosaurs went extinct 65 million years ago.

Crocodiles seem to heal easily after they get hurt. They can live for many years after losing a leg or part of their jaw in a fight. Crocodiles also have the most advanced brain of all reptiles. They're very smart and quickly learn to avoid danger.

CROCODILES HAVE GREAT HEARING AND AN EXCELLENT SENSE OF SMELL. THEY CAN ALSO SEE VERY WELL UNDERWATER AND IN THE DARK.

FOOD FOR LIFE

Crocodiles also adapted to use food **efficiently**. Their stomach can break down feathers, shells, and even bones. They can eat pretty much anything!

Warm-blooded animals need to eat all the time to keep up their inner body temperature. But cold-blooded crocodiles warm up in the sun and cool off in the water to get their body temperature just right to eat and grow. However, in low temperatures, their body functions slow, so they can survive for long periods with little food.

THE PREHISTORIC WORLD

Scientists think some prehistoric crocodiles had hooves and others might have climbed trees!

WHAT'S NEXT?

Crocodiles are true masters of survival, outlasting the most terrible dinosaurs. We can learn a lot about the prehistoric world by studying these ancient creatures. They have another enemy, though: people! People hunt crocodiles for their skin, even though it's against the law. They're also destroying the places where crocodiles live. As a result, some kinds of crocodiles are now in danger of dying out.

Crocodiles have lived on Earth for 200 million years. Are they adapted for the future, too?

WE CAN'T KNOW WHICH ADAPTATIONS HELPED CROCODILES ESCAPE EXTINCTION. LIKELY, IT WAS A COMBINATION.

GLOSSARY

adapt: to change to fit new conditions

cold-blooded: having a body temperature that's the same as the temperature of the surroundings

crocodilian: one of a group of reptiles that includes crocodiles, alligators, caimans, and gharials

efficiently: done in the quickest, best way possible

environment: everything that is around a living thing

evolve: to change over many years

fossil: the hardened marks or remains of plants and animals that formed over thousands or millions of years

gland: a body part that produces something needed for a bodily function

jaw: the bones that hold the teeth and make up the mouth

prehistoric: before recorded history

related: belonging to the same group or family because of shared features

swamp: an area with trees that is covered with water at least part of the time

temperature: how hot or cold something is

FOR MORE INFORMATION

BOOKS

Bodden, Valerie. *Crocodiles*. Mankato, MN: Creative Education, 2010.

Jackson, Tom. *Saltwater Crocodile*. New York, NY: Bearport Publishing, 2014.

Shea, Therese. *Crocodiles*. New York, NY: PowerKids Press, 2015.

WEBSITES

Crocodile Facts for Kids
crocodilefacts.weebly.com/crocodile-facts-for-kids.html
Check out this website for more fun facts about crocodiles.

Did Crocodiles Descend from Dinosaurs?
animals.howstuffworks.com/reptiles/crocodiles-descend-from-dinosaurs.htm
Find out more about the relationship between crocodiles and dinosaurs here.

Publisher's note to educators and parents: Our editors have carefully reviewed these websites to ensure that they are suitable for students. Many websites change frequently, however, and we cannot guarantee that a site's future contents will continue to meet our high standards of quality and educational value. Be advised that students should be closely supervised whenever they access the Internet.

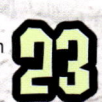

INDEX

adaptation 16, 18, 20, 21
American crocodile 10
archosaurs 6
babies 14, 15
birds 6, 12
brain 16
carnivores 12
crocodilians 6
Deinosuchus 4, 5
eggs 6, 14, 15
enemy 20
fossils 8, 10, 14
glands 10

jaws 8, 12, 16
legs 8, 16
Mourasuchus 12
nest 15
prey 12
Protosuchus 19
reptiles 6, 16
Rhamphosuchus 10
Sarcosuchus 8, 9, 12, 14
snout 8, 10
species 8
tail 8, 10
teeth 4, 8, 14